Complete

SEO

Course

Author RJ ASIM

Annotated by muhamad waqas

Chapter 4: *Off-Page Optimization*

Link building strategies

Social media marketing

Online directories and listings

Influencer marketing

Chapter 5: *Technical SEO*

Understanding website architecture

Site speed optimization

Schema markup

XML sitemap creation and submission

HTTPS implementation

Chapter 6: *Local SEO*

Importance of local SEO for small businesses

Creating and optimizing Google My Business listing

Local keyword research

Creating SEO reports

Chapter 10: Advanced SEO Techniques

Advanced keyword research strategies

Semantic search and latent semantic indexing (LSI)

Voice search optimization

Machine learning and AI in SEO

Future of SEO

Chapter 11: Common SEO Mistakes to Avoid

Keyword stuffing

Duplicate content

Ignoring mobile optimization

Neglecting user experience

Black hat SEO techniques

Chapter 12: Conclusion

Recap of key SEO concepts

Importance of ongoing SEO efforts

Staying up-to-date with SEO trends and changes

. . . .

Chapter 1: Introduction to SEO

SEO stands for Search Engine Optimization, and it

refers to the practice of optimizing your website to

improve its visibility and ranking in search engine
results pages (SERPs). Essentially, the goal of SEO is to
make it easier for people to find your website when
they search for relevant keywords or phrases on search
engines like Google, Bing, or Yahoo.
There are several strategies that can be used to optimize
a website for search engines, including keyword research,
on page optimization, link building, and technical SEO.
Keyword research involves identifying the most relevant

and valuable keywords for your website and incorporating

them into your content in a way that feels natural and

informative. On page optimization refers to optimizing
individual pages on your website for specific keywords
or phrases, while link building involves building high quality

backlinks to your website from other authoritative websites.
Technical SEO focuses on the technical aspects of your website,

such as website speed, mobile optimization, and website

architecture.

By implementing these strategies and optimizing your website

for search engines, you can improve your website's visibility and

ranking in search engine results pages, which can ultimately drive
more traffic to your website and help you achieve your business
goals.

Understanding the basics of SEO

Understanding the basics of SEO can be helpful for anyone who wants to improve the visibility and ranking of their website in search engine results pages.

At its core, SEO involves optimizing your website and its content to make it more attractive to search engines. This can involve a variety of strategies, including:

Keyword research: Identifying the most relevant and valuable keywords and phrases for your website, and incorporating them into your content in a way that feels natural and informative.

On-page optimization: Optimizing individual pages on your website for specific keywords or phrases, including meta tags, headers, and content.

Link building: Building high-quality backlinks to your website from other authoritative websites, which can help to establish your website as a trusted and valuable resource.

Technical SEO: Focusing on the technical aspects of your website, including website speed, mobile optimization, and website architecture.

Content creation: Creating high-quality, informative, and engaging content that is optimized for both search engines and human readers.

Ultimately, the goal of SEO is to improve the visibility and ranking of your website in search engine results pages, which can help to drive more traffic to your website and improve your overall online presence. While SEO can be complex and time-consuming, it can also be highly effective when done correctly, and can help you achieve your business goals and reach your target audience online.

The importance of SEO in online marketing

SEO is an essential aspect of online marketing as it plays a crucial role in increasing the visibility and ranking of a website on search engine results pages. Here are some key reasons why SEO is important in online marketing:

Increased website traffic: By optimizing your website for search engines, you can improve your website's visibility and ranking

, which can ultimately drive more traffic to your website. This increased traffic can lead to more conversions, sales, and revenue for your business.

Cost-effective: SEO can be a cost-effective marketing strategy compared to other forms of online advertising such as paid search ads. Although it may take some time and effort to implement, the results of SEO can be long-lasting and provide a solid return on investment.

Better user experience: By optimizing your website for search engines, you are also optimizing it for your visitors. This can include improving website speed, mobile optimization, and user-friendly navigation, which can all contribute to a better user experience and increase the likelihood of visitors staying on your website longer and returning in the future.

Competitive advantage: SEO can help to establish your website as a valuable and authoritative resource in your industry or niche. By outranking your competitors on search engine results pages, you can gain a competitive advantage and attract more potential customers.

Measurable results: SEO provides measurable results through tools such as Google Analytics. This means you can track your website's performance and make data-driven decisions about how to optimize your website further for better results.

Overall, SEO is an important component of online marketing, and its benefits can have a significant impact on the success and growth of your business. By investing in SEO, you can improve your website's visibility and ranking, attract more potential customers, and ultimately achieve your business goals.

How search engines work

Search engines work by using algorithms to analyze and index the vast amount of information available on the internet, and then provide users with relevant and useful search results based on their search queries. Here's a simplified overview of how search engines work:

Crawling: Search engines use bots, also known as spiders or crawlers, to navigate and explore websites across the internet. These bots crawl websites and follow links from one page to another, gathering information about the content and structure of each page.

Indexing: Once the bots have crawled a website, the search engine will index the pages based on the content and other factors such as

keywords, titles, meta tags, and links. This creates a searchable

database of indexed pages that can be used to provide search

results to users.

Ranking: When a user enters a search query into the search engine

the search engine's algorithm will analyze the indexed pages and

rank them based on their relevance and usefulness to the user's

query. The ranking factors can vary depending on the search engine

but typically include factors such as keyword relevance, content

quality, website authority, and user experience.

Displaying search results: The search engine will display the search

results on a search engine results page (SERP), with the most relevant

and useful results at the top of the page. The user can then click on

the search results to visit the website.

Search engines are constantly updating and refining their algorithms

to provide the most relevant and useful search results to users. By

understanding how search engines work, website owners can

optimize their websites to improve their visibility and ranking

in search engine results pages.

Chapter 2: Keyword Research

Keyword research is the process of identifying and analyzing the words and phrases that people use to search for information on search engines . This research can help website owners and marketers create content that is optimized for relevant keywords, which can improve their website's visibility and ranking in search engine results pages. Here are some key steps involved in keyword research:

Brainstorming: Start by brainstorming a list of potential keywords or phrases that are relevant to your business or industry. Consider what your target audience might be searching for when looking for information related to your products or services.

Keyword research tools: Use keyword research tools such as Google Keyword Planner, SEMrush, or Ahrefs to find additional keyword ideas and insights. These tools can provide information about search volume, competition, and related keywords.

Analyzing competition: Analyze the keywords that your competitors are targeting, and identify any gaps or opportunities where you can target keywords that they are not.

Long-tail keywords: Consider targeting long-tail keywords, which

are longer and more specific phrases that often have less competition

but may have lower search volume.

User intent: Consider the user intent behind each keyword and how it relates to your business. Keywords that are closely aligned with your products or services and user intent can be more valuable to target.

Refining your list: Refine your keyword list based on search volume, competition, relevance, and user intent. Focus on targeting keywords that are the most valuable and relevant to your business.

Keyword research is an ongoing process that requires monitoring and adjustment over time. By regularly analyzing your keyword performance and making adjustments as needed, you can continually improve your website's visibility and ranking in search engine results pages.

Defining your target audience

Defining your target audience is a critical step in any marketing strategy, including SEO. Your target audience is the group of people who are most likely to be interested in your products or services, and who are most likely to become your customers. Here are some key steps involved in defining your target audience:

Analyze your current customers: Start by analyzing your current customer base and identifying common characteristics such as age, gender, location, interests, and behaviors.

14

Conduct market research: Conduct market research to gain insights into your target audience's needs, preferences, and behaviors. This can include surveys, focus groups, and social media listening.

Analyze your competitors: Analyze your competitors' target audience and identify any gaps or opportunities in the market.

Create buyer personas: Create buyer personas, which are fictional representations of your ideal customers based on demographic and psychographic information. This can help you better understand your target audience and tailor your content and messaging to their needs and interests.

Refine your target audience: Refine your target audience based on your research and analysis, and focus on targeting the audience segments that are the most valuable and relevant to your business.

By defining your target audience, you can create SEO strategies and content that are tailored to their needs and interests, which can improve your website's visibility and ranking in search engine results pages.

Using keyword research tools

Keyword research tools can provide valuable insights into the words and phrases that people use to search for information on search engines. These tools can help website owners and marketers identify relevant and high-value keywords to target in their SEO strategies. Here are some common keyword research tools and how to use them:

Google Keyword Planner: This is a free tool provided by Google Ads that provides keyword ideas and insights into search volume, competition, and bid estimates. To use this tool, enter a keyword or phrase related to your business or industry, and the tool will generate a list of related keywords and their performance metrics.

SEMrush: This is a paid tool that provides comprehensive keyword research, competitor analysis, and SEO insights. To use this tool, enter a keyword or domain related to your business or industry, and the tool will generate a list of related keywords, their search volume, competition, and other metrics.

Ahrefs: This is another paid tool that provides comprehensive keyword research, competitor analysis, and SEO insights. To use this tool, enter a keyword or domain related to your business or industry, and the tool will generate a list of related keywords, their search volume, competition, and other metrics.

Keywordtool.io: This is a free or paid tool that provides keyword ideas and insights into search volume, competition, and long-tail keywords. To use this tool, enter a keyword or phrase related to your business or industry, and the tool will generate a list of related keywords and their performance metrics.

When using keyword research tools, it's important to focus on keywords that are relevant to your business and your target audience. Look for keywords with high search volume and low competition, and consider targeting long-tail keywords that are more specific and targeted to your audience. By using keyword research tools effectively, you can identify high-value keywords to target in your SEO strategies, which can improve your website's visibility and ranking in search engine results pages.

Analyzing and selecting keywords

Analyzing and selecting keywords is a crucial part of any SEO strategy. Here are some key steps involved in analyzing and selecting keywords:

Analyze search volume: Use keyword research tools to analyze the search volume for each keyword. Look for keywords with high search volume, as they are likely to drive more traffic to your website.

Evaluate competition: Evaluate the competition for each keyword. Look for keywords with low competition, as they will be easier to rank for and can help improve your website's visibility in search engine results pages.

Consider user intent: Consider the user intent behind each keyword. Look for keywords that align with the intent of your target audience and your business. Keywords that are closely aligned with your products or services and user intent can be more valuable to target.

Focus on long-tail keywords: Focus on targeting long-tail keywords, which are longer and more specific phrases that often have less competition but may have lower search volume. These keywords can help you target specific niches and attract more qualified traffic to your website.

Consider your content strategy: Consider your content strategy when selecting keywords. Look for keywords that align with the content on your website and that you can naturally incorporate into your content.

Refine your list: Refine your keyword list based on search volume, competition, relevance, and user intent. Focus on targeting keywords that are the most valuable and relevant to your business.

When selecting keywords, it's important to prioritize quality over quantity. By targeting relevant and high-value keywords, you can attract more qualified traffic to your website and improve your website's visibility and ranking in search engine results pages. Regularly analyzing your keyword performance and making adjustments as needed can help you continually improve your SEO strategy and attract more traffic to your website.

Creating a keyword strategy

Creating a keyword strategy is a crucial part of any SEO strategy. Here are some key steps involved in creating a keyword strategy:

Define your goals: Start by defining your SEO goals. What are you hoping to achieve with your SEO strategy? Are you looking to increase website traffic, generate more leads, or boost conversions? Defining your goals will help you focus your keyword strategy and ensure that it aligns with your overall business objectives.

Define your target audience: Define your target audience and consider their interests, preferences, and search behavior. This will help you identify the keywords and phrases they are likely to use when searching for products or services related to your business.

Conduct keyword research: Use keyword research tools to identify relevant and high-value keywords that align with your business and target audience. Look for keywords with high search volume and low competition, and consider targeting long-tail keywords that are more specific and targeted to your audience.

Group keywords into themes: Group your keywords into themes based on relevance and intent. This will help you organize your keyword strategy and ensure that you are targeting the right keywords for each page of your website.

Map keywords to content: Map your keywords to specific pages or sections of your website. This will help you create targeted and relevant content that aligns with your keyword strategy and meets the needs of your target audience.

Monitor and adjust your strategy: Regularly monitor your keyword performance and adjust your strategy as needed. This will help you optimize your keyword strategy over time and ensure that you are targeting the most valuable and relevant keywords for your business.

By creating a comprehensive keyword strategy, you can improve your website's visibility and ranking in search engine results pages, attract more qualified traffic to your website, and achieve your SEO goals.

Chapter 3: On-Page Optimizatio

On-page optimization refers to the process of optimizing individual web pages to improve their visibility and ranking in search engine results pages. On-page optimization includes a variety of techniques, such as optimizing content, metadata, and internal linking, to make your web pages more search engine friendly.

Here are some key on-page optimization techniques:

Keyword optimization: Include your target keywords in your page title, meta description, header tags, and throughout your content. However, avoid keyword stuffing as it can negatively impact your ranking.

Content optimization: Create high-quality, relevant, and unique content that provides value to your audience. Use descriptive and engaging titles, headers, and subheadings to make your content more readable and engaging.

Metadata optimization: Write unique and descriptive title tags and meta descriptions that accurately describe the content on your web page. This helps search engines understand what your page is about and can improve click-through rates.

Internal linking: Link to other relevant pages on your website to help search engines understand the structure of your website and improve navigation for users.

Image optimization: Optimize images on your website by compressing them for faster loading times, using descriptive file names, and adding alt text tags that describe the content of the image.

Mobile optimization: Ensure that your website is mobile-friendly and optimized for different devices and screen sizes. This is particularly important as more and more users are accessing the internet from mobile devices.

By implementing these on-page optimization techniques, you can improve the visibility and ranking of your web pages in search engine results pages, attract more traffic to your website, and provide a better user experience for your audience.

Optimizing your website's contennt

Optimizing your website's content is an essential part of on-page optimization. Here are some key tips for optimizing your website's content:

Use relevant and targeted keywords: Include your target keywords in your content, but avoid keyword stuffing. Focus on creating high-quality, relevant, and engaging content that provides value to your audience.

Write compelling titles and headers: Use descriptive and engaging titles and headers to make your content more readable and engaging. This can help improve click-through rates and keep users engaged with your content.

Optimize your meta descriptions: Write unique and descriptive meta descriptions that accurately describe the content on your web page. This can improve click-through rates and help search engines understand the relevance of your content.

Use internal linking: Link to other relevant pages on your website to help search engines understand the structure of your website and improve navigation for users.

Create high-quality content: Focus on creating high-quality, relevant, and unique content that provides value to your audience. Use descriptive and engaging titles, headers, and subheadings to make your content more readable and engaging.

Use multimedia: Incorporate multimedia such as images, videos, and infographics into your content to make it more engaging and shareable.

Optimize for readability: Use short paragraphs, bullet points, and subheadings to make your content more readable and scannable. This can improve user engagement and keep users on your website longer.

By optimizing your website's content, you can improve the visibility and ranking of your web pages in search engine results pages, attract more traffic to your website, and provide a better user experience for your audience.

Creating title tags and meta descriptions

Creating effective title tags and meta descriptions is a crucial part of on-page optimization. Here are some tips for creating title tags and meta descriptions that are both search engine friendly and compelling for users:

Title tags:

Use relevant keywords: Include your target keywords in your title tag, but avoid keyword stuffing. Focus on creating a title tag that accurately describes the content on your web page.

Keep it short: Keep your title tag under 60 characters to ensure it doesn't get truncated in search engine results pages.

Make it engaging: Use descriptive and engaging language that entices users to click through to your web page.

Include your brand name: Include your brand name in your title tag to build brand recognition and trust with your audience.

Meta descriptions:

Use relevant keywords: Include your target keywords in your meta description, but avoid keyword stuffing. Focus on creating a meta description that accurately describes the content on your web page.

Keep it short: Keep your meta description under 155 characters to ensure it doesn't get truncated in search engine results pages.

Make it engaging: Use descriptive and engaging language that entices users to click through to your web page.

Include a call-to-action: Include a call-to-action in your meta description, such as "Learn more" or "Get started today", to encourage users to take action.

It's important to note that title tags and meta descriptions should be unique for each web page on your website. By creating compelling and optimized title tags and meta descriptions, you can improve click-through rates, attract more traffic to your website, and provide a better user experience for your audience.

Internal linking and site structure

Internal linking and site structure are essential aspects of on-page optimization. Here's what you need to know:

Internal linking:

Internal linking is the practice of linking to other pages on your website from within your content. This helps search engines understand the structure of your website and the relevance of your content. Internal linking also provides a better user experience by helping users navigate your website and find relevant information.

Here are some tips for internal linking:

Use descriptive anchor text: Use descriptive and relevant anchor text when linking to other pages on your website. This helps search engines understand the relevance of the linked page.

Link to relevant pages: Link to other relevant pages on your website that provide additional value to your audience.

Use a logical structure: Use a logical site structure to help users navigate your website and find relevant information.

Site structure:

Site structure refers to the organization and hierarchy of your website's pages. A well-organized site structure can help search engines understand the relevance and importance of your content, as well as improve navigation for users.

Here are some tips for site structure:

Use a clear hierarchy: Use a clear hierarchy of pages that logically organize your content. This can help search engines understand the relevance and importance of your content.

Use breadcrumb navigation: Use breadcrumb navigation to help users understand their current location on your website and easily navigate to higher-level pages.

Create a sitemap: Create a sitemap that outlines the structure of your website and provides search engines with an easy-to-follow map of your pages.

By optimizing your internal linking and site structure, you can improve the visibility and ranking of your web pages in search engine results pages, attract more traffic to your website, and provide a better user experience for your audience.

Optimizing images and videos

Optimizing images and videos is an important aspect of on-page optimization that can improve the user experience and search engine visibility of your web pages. Here are some tips for optimizing images and videos:

Images:

Choose the right file format: Use the right file format for your images, such as JPEG for photographs and PNG for graphics with transparent backgrounds.

Compress your images: Compress your images to reduce their file size and improve page load times.

Use descriptive filenames: Use descriptive and relevant filenames for your images that include your target keywords, such as "blue-widget.jpg".

Use alt tags: Use alt tags to describe your images to search engines and improve accessibility for users.

Videos:

Host your videos on a reliable platform: Host your videos on a reliable platform such as YouTube or Vimeo to ensure fast and reliable playback.

Use descriptive titles and descriptions: Use descriptive titles and descriptions for your videos that include your target keywords.

Include transcripts and captions: Include transcripts and captions for your videos to improve accessibility for users and provide search engines with more information about the content of your videos.

By optimizing your images and videos, you can improve the user experience on your web pages, reduce page load times, and improve the search engine visibility of your content.

Mobile optimization

Mobile optimization is the process of ensuring that your website is optimized for mobile devices such as smartphones and tablets. As more and more users access the internet on mobile devices, mobile optimization has become an essential aspect of on-page optimization. Here are some tips for mobile optimization:

Use a responsive design: Use a responsive design that automatically adjusts the layout and content of your website to fit the screen size of the device being used.

Optimize page load times: Mobile users expect fast load times, so optimize your website's performance by compressing images and minimizing the use of large files and plugins.

Use legible fonts: Use fonts that are legible on small screens and ensure that your font size is large enough to be easily read on mobile devices.

Use a mobile-friendly navigation: Use a navigation that is optimized for mobile devices, such as a hamburger menu or collapsible menu.

Optimize forms: Optimize any forms on your website for mobile devices, such as reducing the number of fields or using larger form fields for touch input.

Use mobile-friendly media: Ensure that any images or videos on your website are optimized for mobile devices and can be easily viewed and navigated on small screens.

By optimizing your website for mobile devices, you can improve the user experience for mobile users, increase engagement and conversions, and improve your search engine rankings.

Chapter 4: Off-Page Optimization

Off-page optimization refers to the activities that you do outside of your own website to improve its search engine rankings and visibility. Here are some important strategies for off-page optimization:

Link building: Building high-quality backlinks from other websites to your own is one of the most important off-page optimization strategies. This helps to increase your website's authority and relevance in the eyes of search engines.

Social media marketing: Social media platforms provide an opportunity to engage with your audience, share your content, and drive traffic back to your website. Social media activity can also indirectly influence your search engine rankings.

Influencer marketing: Partnering with influencers or other authoritative websites in your industry can help to increase your website's visibility and attract high-quality backlinks.

Guest blogging: Writing and publishing articles on other websites in your industry can help to establish your expertise and attract backlinks to your own website.

Local SEO: If you have a local business, optimizing your website for local search is important. This involves optimizing your website for local keywords and directories, and managing your online reputation on local review sites.

By incorporating these off-page optimization strategies into your overall SEO strategy, you can improve your website's search engine visibility, drive more traffic to your website, and increase your online authority and reputation.

Link building strategies

Link building is the process of acquiring backlinks from other websites to your own. Here are some effective link building strategies:

Create high-quality content: Creating high-quality, informative, and engaging content is one of the best ways to attract backlinks naturally. People are more likely to link to content that they find useful or interesting.

Guest blogging: Writing guest posts for other blogs in your industry is a great way to get your content in front of a new audience and attract backlinks. Make sure to choose blogs with high authority and relevance to your niche.

Broken link building: This involves finding broken links on other websites in your industry and offering to replace them with relevant links to your own content. This benefits both the website owner and you by providing a solution for the broken link and a new backlink for your website.

Resource link building: Creating comprehensive resources such as guides, tutorials, or infographics can attract backlinks from other websites that find your content valuable and relevant.

Competitor analysis: Analyzing the backlink profiles of your competitors can help you identify potential link building opportunities that you may have overlooked. You can also reach out to websites that link to your competitors and offer them better content or more value to attract backlinks to your own website.

It's important to remember that the quality of the backlinks is more important than the quantity. Focus on acquiring high-quality backlinks from authoritative and relevant websites in your industry.

Social media marketing

Social media marketing involves using social media platforms to promote your brand, engage with your audience, and drive traffic to your website. Here are some strategies for effective social media marketing:

Choose the right platforms: Identify the social media platforms that are most relevant to your target audience and focus your efforts on those platforms. For example, if you are targeting a younger audience, Instagram or TikTok may be more effective than LinkedIn.

Create engaging content: Create content that is engaging, informative, and visually appealing. This can include images, videos, infographics, or written content.

Consistency is key: Consistency is important for building a strong presence on social media. Post regularly and at the right time for your audience to increase engagement and reach.

Use hashtags: Use relevant hashtags to increase the visibility of your content and make it easier for people to find you. Do some research to identify popular and relevant hashtags in your industry.

Engage with your audience: Respond to comments, messages, and mentions on social media to build relationships with your audience and increase engagement.

Use paid advertising: Social media platforms offer a range of advertising options to help you reach a wider audience and drive traffic to your website. Consider investing in paid advertising if you have the budget.

By implementing these social media marketing strategies, you can increase your brand awareness, engagement, and website traffic.

Online directories and listings

Online directories and listings are websites that list businesses and their information, such as name, address, phone number, and website URL. These directories can be general or specific to certain industries or locations.

Here are some benefits of being listed on online directories:

Increased visibility: Being listed on online directories can increase your business's visibility online, making it easier for potential customers to find you.

Improved search engine rankings: Many online directories have high authority and are frequently crawled by search engines. Being listed on these directories can improve your search engine rankings and drive more traffic to your website.

Local SEO: Local directories, such as Google My Business and Yelp, can help improve your local SEO by providing relevant and accurate information to local searchers.

Reputation management: Online directories allow customers to leave reviews and ratings of your business. Positive reviews can help improve your reputation and attract new customers.

Here are some tips for optimizing your online directory listings:

Consistency: Ensure that your business information is consistent across all online directories to avoid confusion and improve your search engine rankings.

Accuracy: Keep your business information up-to-date and accurate to avoid customer frustration and confusion.

Complete profiles: Fill out your business profile on each directory completely, including photos, descriptions, and categories.

Monitor reviews: Respond to both positive and negative reviews promptly to show that you value customer feedback and improve your reputation.

By being listed on relevant online directories and optimizing your listings, you can improve your online visibility, reputation, and search engine rankings.

Influencer marketing

Influencer marketing is a form of marketing that involves partnering with social media influencers to promote your products or services to their followers. Influencers are individuals with a large following on social media platforms such as Instagram, YouTube, and TikTok, and they can have a significant impact on their followers' purchasing decisions.

Here are some benefits of influencer marketing:

Increased credibility: Influencers have built trust with their followers, and partnering with them can increase your brand's credibility and reputation.

Expanded reach: Influencers have large followings, and partnering with them can help you reach a wider audience.

Targeted audience: You can choose influencers who have followers in your target audience to ensure that your message reaches the right people.

Authentic content: Influencers create authentic and engaging content that resonates with their followers, making it more likely that they will engage with your brand.

Here are some tips for effective influencer marketing:

Choose the right influencers: Choose influencers who align with your brand values and have a following that matches your target audience.

Develop a strong partnership: Develop a strong partnership with the influencer and work together to create content that resonates with their followers and promotes your brand.

Provide creative freedom: Allow the influencer creative freedom to ensure that the content they create is authentic and engaging.

Measure success: Track the success of your influencer marketing campaigns to determine their effectiveness and make adjustments as needed.

By partnering with the right influencers and developing strong partnerships, you can increase your brand's reach, credibility, and engagement.

Chapter 5: Technical SEO

Technical SEO refers to the optimization of your website's technical elements to improve your search engine rankings and user experience. Here are some key technical SEO elements:

Website speed: Website speed is an important ranking factor and affects user experience. Optimize your website's speed by compressing images, minimizing code, and using a content delivery network (CDN).

Mobile responsiveness: With the majority of internet users accessing websites on mobile devices, it's important to have a mobile-responsive website. Use a responsive design that adjusts to different screen sizes.

Site structure: A well-organized site structure makes it easier for search engines to crawl your website and understand its content. Use a logical hierarchy with clear categories and subcategories.

URL structure: Use descriptive, short, and readable URLs that include relevant keywords to help search engines and users understand the content of the page.

Sitemap: A sitemap is a file that lists all the pages on your website and helps search engines crawl and index them. Submit a sitemap to search engines to improve your website's visibility.

Robots.txt: A robots.txt file tells search engines which pages to crawl and which to ignore. Use this file to prevent search engines from crawling duplicate content or sensitive pages.

Schema markup: Schema markup is code added to your website that helps search engines understand the content of your pages. Use schema markup to improve your website's visibility and click-through rates.

By optimizing these technical elements, you can improve your website's search engine rankings, user experience, and overall performance.

Understanding website architecture

Website architecture refers to the way your website is structured and organized, including the hierarchy of pages, menus, and navigation. A well-organized website architecture makes it easier for search engines to crawl and understand your website, improving your search engine rankings and user experience.

Here are some key elements of website architecture:

Hierarchy: Your website should have a clear hierarchy, with the most important pages at the top and lesser pages below. Use clear categories and subcategories to organize your pages.

Navigation: Your website's navigation should be easy to use and intuitive, with clear menus and links to important pages.

Internal linking: Internal linking refers to the links between pages on your website. Use internal links to help users navigate your website and to help search engines understand the relationships between your pages.

URL structure: Use descriptive, short, and readable URLs that include relevant keywords to help search engines and users understand the content of the page.

Site maps: A site map is a file that lists all the pages on your website and helps search engines crawl and index them. Submit a site map to search engines to improve your website's visibility.

Page speed: Website speed is an important ranking factor and affects user experience. Optimize your website's speed by compressing images, minimizing code, and using a content delivery network (CDN).

By organizing your website's architecture effectively, you can improve your website's search engine rankings and user experience, making it easier for users to navigate your website and find the information they need.

Site speed optimization

Site speed optimization refers to the process of improving the loading speed of your website. A faster website not only provides a better user experience, but also improves your search engine rankings. Here are some ways to optimize your website's speed:

Compress images: Large image files can slow down your website's loading time. Use image compression tools to reduce the file size of your images without compromising quality.

Minimize HTTP requests: Every time a web page is loaded, the browser sends an HTTP request for each file on the page, including images, scripts, and stylesheets. Minimize the number of HTTP requests by reducing the number of files and combining them into a single file.

Enable caching: Caching temporarily stores website data on a user's computer, making it faster to load the website on subsequent visits. Enable browser caching and server-side caching to improve website speed.

Minimize code: Remove unnecessary code and whitespace to reduce the file size of your website's HTML, CSS, and JavaScript files.

Use a content delivery network (CDN): A CDN is a network of servers that store copies of your website's files in multiple locations. By using a CDN, you can reduce the distance between your website and the user, improving loading times.

Optimize your hosting: Choose a reliable web hosting provider with fast servers and a good uptime guarantee. Upgrade to a better hosting plan if necessary to improve website speed.

By optimizing your website's speed, you can improve your search engine rankings and provide a better user experience for your visitors.

Schema markup

Schema markup is a type of structured data that is added to a website's HTML code to provide more information about the content on the page. This information can be used by search engines to better understand the content and display relevant information in search results.

Schema markup uses a set of standardized tags to describe various types of content, such as articles, reviews, events, products, and more. Some examples of the types of information that can be included in schema markup include:

Name and description of the content

Date and time of an event

Price and availability of a product

Ratings and reviews of a business or product

Contact information for a business

By using schema markup, website owners can provide more detailed and accurate information to search engines, which can lead to improved search rankings and more relevant search results for users. Schema markup can also be used to enhance the appearance of search results by displaying rich snippets, such as star ratings, images, and additional information about the content on the page.

Schema markup can be added to a website's HTML code manually or with the help of plugins or tools. It is important to follow the guidelines set by schema.org to ensure that the markup is properly formatted and recognized by search engines.

XML sitemap creation and submission

An XML sitemap is a file that lists all the pages on a website that a search engine should index. It helps search engines crawl and understand the structure of a website, making it easier for them to index the site's content.

Creating and submitting an XML sitemap involves the following steps:

Create an XML sitemap: There are several online tools and plugins that can help you create an XML sitemap for your website. Alternatively, you can create one manually using a text editor or an XML editor.

Add the sitemap to your website: Once you have created the XML sitemap, you need to add it to your website's root directory. You can do this manually using FTP or a file manager, or by using a plugin or tool.

Notify search engines: You need to notify search engines that you have created an XML sitemap and provide them with the URL of the sitemap file. You can do this by submitting the sitemap to the search engine's webmaster tools or by adding the sitemap URL to the robots.txt file.

Submitting an XML sitemap can help ensure that all the important pages on your website are indexed by search engines. It can also help search engines understand the structure of your website and prioritize the most important pages for indexing.

HTTPS implementation

HTTPS (Hypertext Transfer Protocol Secure) is a secure version of HTTP that encrypts data sent between a website and a user's browser. Implementing HTTPS on your website is important for several reasons, including improved security, privacy, and SEO.

To implement HTTPS on your website, you need to obtain an SSL (Secure Sockets Layer) certificate from a trusted certificate authority. There are several types of SSL certificates available, including single-domain, multi-domain, and wildcard certificates.

Once you have obtained an SSL certificate, you need to install it on your web server and configure your website to use HTTPS instead of HTTP. This typically involves updating your website's configuration files and/or using plugins or tools to redirect all HTTP requests to HTTPS.

After you have implemented HTTPS, you should test your website to ensure that all pages and resources are properly secured and there are no mixed content warnings. You should also update any internal links, redirects, and third-party integrations to use HTTPS URLs.

Implementing HTTPS can have several benefits for your website, including improved security, privacy, and trustworthiness for your users. It can also help improve your website's SEO by providing a secure and encrypted connection for users and by being a ranking factor in Google's search algorithm.

Chapter 6: Local SEO

Local SEO is the practice of optimizing a website to improve its visibility and ranking in local search results. Local search results are those that are relevant to a user's location, such as when they search for "restaurants near me" or "dentists in [city]".

Optimizing a website for local SEO involves several strategies, including:

Claiming and optimizing Google My Business (GMB) listing: A GMB listing is a free business listing on Google that displays information about a business, such as its address, phone number, website, reviews, and photos. Optimizing a GMB listing involves providing accurate and detailed information, adding photos and videos, and responding to reviews.

Building local citations: Local citations are mentions of a business's name, address, and phone number (NAP) on other websites, such as online directories, review sites, and social media platforms. Building local citations helps improve a business's visibility and credibility in local search results.

Obtaining local backlinks: Backlinks are links from other websites to a business's website. Obtaining local backlinks from other local businesses, organizations, and media outlets can help improve a business's local search ranking.

Optimizing website content for local keywords: Optimizing website content for local keywords, such as "[service] in [city]", can help improve a website's visibility in local search results.

Encouraging customer reviews: Customer reviews are a signal of a business's reputation and credibility. Encouraging customers to leave reviews on GMB and other review sites can help improve a business's local search ranking.

Implementing local SEO strategies can help improve a business's visibility and ranking in local search results, leading to increased website traffic, leads, and sales from local customers.

Importance of local SEO for small businesses

Local SEO is particularly important for small businesses because it helps them to compete with larger businesses that have a national or global presence. By focusing on local search results, small businesses can reach potential customers in their immediate area who are actively searching for the products or services they offer.

Here are some specific reasons why local SEO is important for small businesses:

Increased visibility: Local SEO can help small businesses appear higher in local search results, increasing their visibility to potential customers who are actively searching for products or services in their area.

More targeted traffic: Local SEO can help small businesses attract more targeted traffic to their website. This is because people who are searching for local businesses are often looking to make a purchase or hire a service provider, making them more likely to convert into customers.

Improved reputation: Local SEO strategies such as obtaining customer reviews can help small businesses build a positive reputation in their community. This can lead to increased trust and credibility, which can in turn lead to more customers and sales.

Cost-effective: Local SEO can be a cost-effective way for small businesses to reach potential customers in their area. Compared to traditional forms of advertising, such as print or radio ads, local SEO strategies can be more affordable and offer a better return on investment.

Overall, local SEO is a powerful tool for small businesses looking to grow and succeed in their local market. By implementing local SEO strategies, small businesses can improve their online presence, attract more customers, and compete with larger businesses in their industry.

Creating and optimizing Google My Business listing

Google My Business (GMB) is a free tool that allows businesses to manage their online presence on Google, including their search engine results page (SERP) listing, Google Maps listing, and Google+ page. Optimizing your GMB listing is an important part of local SEO and can help your business to appear higher in local search results.

Here are some steps to create and optimize your GMB listing:

Claim your listing: Go to the Google My Business website and claim your business listing. Verify your business by providing a physical address and phone number.

Complete your profile: Fill out all the required fields in your GMB profile, including your business name, address, phone number, website, hours of operation, and business category. Make sure that your information is accurate and consistent with what is listed on your website and other online directories.

Add photos: Add high-quality photos of your business, including your logo, products or services, and your team. This can help to showcase your business and make it more attractive to potential customers.

Obtain customer reviews: Encourage your customers to leave reviews on your GMB listing. Positive reviews can help to improve your reputation and increase your visibility in local search results.

Use Google Posts: Use the Google Posts feature to share news, promotions, or updates about your business. These posts appear in your GMB listing and can help to attract potential customers.

Monitor your listing: Regularly monitor your GMB listing for any updates or changes. Respond to customer reviews and questions promptly to show that you value their feedback and are committed to providing excellent customer service.

By following these steps and optimizing your GMB listing, you can improve your local SEO and increase your visibility to potential customers in your area.

Local keyword research

When it comes to local SEO, conducting keyword research is important for identifying the search terms that your target audience is using to find businesses like yours in your local area. Here are some tips for conducting local keyword research:

Use location-specific keywords: Include the name of your city, town, or region in your keyword research. For example, if you're a bakery in New York City, target keywords like "New York City bakery" or "best bakeries in NYC".

Research local competitors: Look at the websites and online listings of your local competitors to see what keywords they are targeting. This can help you to identify new opportunities for targeting specific keywords and phrases.

Use keyword research tools: Use tools like Google Keyword Planner or Ahrefs to research keywords related to your business and location. Look for keywords with a high search volume and low competition.

Consider long-tail keywords: Long-tail keywords are longer phrases that are more specific and targeted. For example, instead of targeting "pizza restaurant", target "best thin crust pizza restaurant in Chicago". Long-tail keywords can be less competitive and more likely to convert into customers.

Analyze search intent: Consider the intent behind the search terms you are targeting. Are people searching for information, looking for a specific product or service, or trying to find a location? This can help you to optimize your website and content for the right keywords and improve your chances of ranking in local search results.

By conducting local keyword research, you can identify the most relevant and effective keywords to target for your business, improving your local SEO and helping you to reach more customers in your area.

Building local citations

Local citations are mentions of your business name, address, and phone number (NAP) on other websites, directories, and online listings. Building local citations is an important aspect of local SEO, as it helps to increase your business's visibility and credibility online. Here are some tips for building local citations:

Ensure consistency: It's important to ensure that your NAP information is consistent across all citations. This means that your business name, address, and phone number should be the same on every website and directory where your business is listed.

Claim and optimize listings: Claim and optimize your business listings on popular directories and online listings, such as Google My Business, Yelp, and Facebook. Optimize your listings with accurate and up-to-date information about your business, including your NAP, website URL, and business hours.

Build quality citations: Focus on building citations on high-quality websites and directories that are relevant to your business and location. This can include industry-specific directories, local chamber of commerce websites, and community websites.

Monitor and update: Regularly monitor your business listings and citations to ensure that your NAP information is accurate and up-to-date. Update any incorrect or outdated information as soon as possible to avoid any confusion or misunderstandings.

Use citation tools: There are a number of citation tools available that can help you to build and manage your local citations, such as Moz Local, BrightLocal, and Yext.

By building local citations, you can improve your business's online presence and visibility in local search results, making it easier for potential customers to find and contact your business.

Chapter 7: E-commerce SEO

E-commerce SEO is the practice of optimizing online stores to increase their visibility and rankings on search engine results pages (SERPs). Here are some key strategies for improving e-commerce SEO:

Conduct keyword research: Start by identifying relevant keywords and phrases that potential customers might use to search for products that your online store sells. Use keyword research tools to find relevant search terms and incorporate them into your product descriptions and meta tags.

Optimize product pages: Optimize your product pages by including descriptive product titles, detailed descriptions, high-quality images, and customer reviews. Use schema markup to provide additional information about your products to search engines.

Improve site structure: A well-organized site structure can help search engines to crawl and index your e-commerce store more effectively. Use categories, subcategories, and internal linking to create a logical and intuitive navigation system.

Focus on user experience: A positive user experience is essential for both SEO and conversions. Ensure that your website is mobile-friendly, has a fast loading speed, and is easy to navigate.

Build high-quality backlinks: Backlinks from reputable and relevant websites can help to improve your online store's authority and search engine rankings. Reach out to industry influencers, bloggers, and other websites to request backlinks to your online store.

Leverage social media: Social media can help to drive traffic to your e-commerce store and improve your online presence. Use social media platforms to promote your products, engage with your customers, and build your brand.

By implementing these strategies, you can improve the visibility and rankings of your e-commerce store on search engines, drive more traffic and sales, and ultimately grow your online business.

Product page optimization

Product page optimization is an important aspect of e-commerce SEO that involves optimizing individual product pages to improve their visibility and rankings on search engines. Here are some key strategies for optimizing product pages:

Use descriptive product titles: Use clear and descriptive titles that accurately describe the product and include relevant keywords.

Optimize product descriptions: Use detailed product descriptions that highlight the features and benefits of the product. Use bullet points and subheadings to make the content more scannable and easy to read.

Include high-quality images and videos: Use high-quality images and videos that showcase the product from different angles and provide additional context. Optimize image file names and alt tags with relevant keywords.

Encourage customer reviews: Encourage customers to leave reviews of your products, as these can improve trust and credibility with potential customers and improve rankings on search engines.

Use schema markup: Use schema markup to provide additional information about the product, such as its price, availability, and reviews. This can help to improve visibility on search engines and increase click-through rates.

Optimize meta tags: Use optimized meta titles and descriptions that include relevant keywords and accurately describe the product.

By implementing these strategies, you can improve the visibility and rankings of your product pages on search engines, increase click-through rates, and ultimately drive more sales for your e-commerce store.

Category page optimization

Category page optimization is an important aspect of e-commerce SEO that involves optimizing the pages that display a group of related products. Here are some key strategies for optimizing category pages:

Use descriptive category names: Use clear and descriptive names that accurately describe the category and include relevant keywords.

Optimize category descriptions: Use detailed category descriptions that highlight the features and benefits of the products in that category. Use bullet points and subheadings to make the content more scannable and easy to read.

Include relevant filtering options: Make it easy for users to refine their search by including relevant filtering options, such as price range, color, size, and brand.

Use high-quality images: Use high-quality images to showcase the products in the category. Optimize image file names and alt tags with relevant keywords.

Include links to relevant subcategories and products: Include links to relevant subcategories and individual products to help users find what they are looking for.

Optimize meta tags: Use optimized meta titles and descriptions that include relevant keywords and accurately describe the category.

By implementing these strategies, you can improve the visibility and rankings of your category pages on search engines, make it easier for users to find what they are looking for, and ultimately drive more sales for your e-commerce store.

Structured data for e-commerce

Structured data is a way to provide search engines with additional information about your website's content, making it easier for them to understand and index it correctly. This is especially important for e-commerce websites, as structured data can help improve the visibility and click-through rates of product listings in search engine results pages (SERPs).

Here are some examples of structured data that can be used for e-commerce:

Product schema: This type of schema is used to provide detailed information about individual products, including their name, brand, description, price, availability, and reviews.

It can also include additional details such as product images, video, and product variations.

Review schema: This type of schema is used to provide additional information about product reviews, including the reviewer's name, rating, and review text.

Breadcrumb schema: This type of schema is used to create a navigation trail that shows where a product is located within the site's hierarchy. This can be especially useful for e-commerce sites that have a large number of product categories.

Organization schema: This type of schema provides information about the organization behind the website, including its name, logo, contact information, and social media profiles.

By implementing structured data on your e-commerce website, you can help search engines better understand and index your content, improve the appearance of your product listings in SERPs, and ultimately drive more traffic and sales to your site.

Building high-quality backlinks for e-commerce

Building high-quality backlinks for e-commerce websites is crucial for improving their search engine rankings and driving more traffic to their online stores. Here are some effective strategies for building backlinks:

Guest posting: Reach out to relevant blogs and websites in your industry and offer to write a guest post for them. In return, you can include a link to your e-commerce site in the author bio or within the article.

Broken link building: Find broken links on relevant websites and offer to replace them with links to your e-commerce site. This helps the website owner by fixing a broken link and helps you by building a high-quality backlink.

Influencer outreach: Reach out to influencers in your industry and ask them to share your e-commerce site with their followers. You can also offer to collaborate on content or promotions to drive more traffic and backlinks.

Resource page link building: Identify relevant resource pages in your industry and reach out to the website owner to request a link to your e-commerce site be added. This can be done by providing useful information or tools that would benefit their audience.

Competitor link analysis: Analyze the backlinks of your competitors and identify opportunities to build similar links for your e-commerce site. This can be done by creating better content or offering unique products or services that are not currently being linked to.

Remember, building high-quality backlinks takes time and effort. It's important to focus on building relationships and providing value to other websites in order to earn backlinks that will have a positive impact on your e-commerce site's search engine rankings.

Chapter 8: Content Marketing

Content marketing is a strategy that involves creating and sharing valuable, relevant, and consistent content to attract and retain a clearly defined audience. This chapter focuses on the role of content marketing in SEO and how it can help to improve search engine rankings.

Content marketing involves creating a wide range of content types such as blog posts, videos, infographics, social media posts, and e-books, among others. The content is usually created to address specific pain points or interests of the target audience. The main aim of content marketing is to build a relationship with the audience, provide them with valuable information, and ultimately influence their purchasing decisions.

In SEO, content marketing plays a crucial role in driving traffic to a website. When people search for information or solutions to their problems, search engines look for relevant content to display in the search results. By creating high-quality content that matches the user's search intent, websites can attract more traffic and increase their visibility in the search results.

Content marketing can also help to improve the website's backlink profile. When people find the content valuable, they are more likely to link back to it from their websites, social media accounts, or other online platforms. This, in turn, can help to improve the website's authority and relevance in the eyes of search engines.

To create an effective content marketing strategy, it is important to conduct keyword research and identify the topics that the target audience is interested in. The content should be optimized for SEO by including relevant keywords in the title, headings, and body of the content. It is also important to ensure that the content is engaging and informative, and that it provides value to the audience.

In summary, content marketing is a powerful tool that can help to improve a website's SEO performance. By creating high-quality content that matches the user's search intent, websites can attract more traffic, improve their visibility in the search results, and build a strong relationship with their audience.

Importance of content in SEO

Content plays a crucial role in SEO as it is one of the primary factors that search engines use to determine the relevance and value of a website. Search engines aim to provide the most relevant and useful results to users, and high-quality content is a significant indicator of a website's relevance and value.

In addition to providing value to users, creating high-quality content on a consistent basis can also help attract backlinks and social shares, which are important factors in improving a website's visibility and authority in search engine results pages. Content can also be optimized for specific keywords and phrases to improve a website's ranking for those terms.

Overall, content is an integral part of any successful SEO strategy, and investing in high-quality, relevant content can lead to long-term success and increased visibility in search results.

Content creation and optimization

Content creation and optimization are essential components of a successful SEO strategy. Here are some tips for creating and optimizing content for SEO:

Conduct keyword research: Keyword research helps you identify the words and phrases that your target audience is searching for. Use this information to inform your content creation process and optimize your content for relevant keywords.

Create high-quality, engaging content: Your content should provide value to your audience and be engaging enough to keep them on your website. Use a mix of text, images, and videos to make your content more engaging and informative.

Optimize your content for SEO: Use relevant keywords in your content, including the title, meta description, headers, and body copy. Use descriptive and unique URLs, and include alt tags for images.

Focus on user experience: Make sure your content is easy to read and navigate, with clear headings and subheadings. Use bullet points and lists to break up your content and make it easier to digest.

Keep your content fresh: Regularly updating your content with new information and insights can help improve its relevance and keep users coming back to your website.

By following these tips, you can create high-quality, optimized content that not only provides value to your audience but also improves your website's visibility and ranking in search engine results pages.

Content promotion and distribution

Content promotion and distribution are crucial parts of any successful content marketing strategy. Once you have created high-quality content, you need to make sure that it reaches your target audience. Here are some ways to promote and distribute your content:

Social Media: Share your content on various social media platforms where your target audience is most active. You can also use social media advertising to reach a larger audience.

Email Marketing: Send your content to your email list and encourage your subscribers to share it with their network.

Influencer Marketing: Reach out to influencers in your niche and ask them to share your content with their followers.

Guest Posting: Write guest posts for relevant websites and include a link back to your content.

Content Syndication: Syndicate your content on platforms like Medium or LinkedIn to reach a wider audience.

Paid Advertising: Use paid advertising platforms like Google Ads or Facebook Ads to promote your content to a specific audience.

Community Engagement: Join online communities where your target audience is active and share your content with them.

By promoting and distributing your content through these channels, you can increase its visibility, reach a larger audience, and ultimately drive more traffic to your website.

Measuring content success

Measuring the success of your content marketing efforts is crucial to understanding what works and what doesn't, allowing you to make data-driven decisions for future campaigns. Here are some key metrics to consider:

Traffic: Monitor the number of visitors to your website, as well as the source of that traffic (organic, social, etc.) to see how your content is driving traffic.

Engagement: Measure the level of engagement with your content, such as likes, shares, comments, and backlinks.

Conversions: Keep track of how many visitors are taking a desired action on your website, such as filling out a contact form or making a purchase.

Time on site: Monitor how long visitors are spending on your site, as well as which pages they are spending the most time on, to gauge the effectiveness of your content in keeping visitors engaged.

Bounce rate: Monitor the percentage of visitors who leave your site after viewing only one page, which can indicate a lack of engagement or relevance.

ROI: Measure the return on investment for your content marketing efforts, taking into account the cost of producing and promoting your content and the revenue generated from resulting conversions.

By tracking and analyzing these metrics, you can gain valuable insights into the effectiveness of your content marketing strategy and make adjustments as needed to improve results.

Chapter 9: Analytics and Reporting

Analyzing your website's data is crucial to understanding how your SEO efforts are performing and making informed decisions on how to improve them. In this chapter, we'll cover the basics of analytics and reporting in SEO.

Understanding Google Analytics

Google Analytics is a free tool that allows you to track and analyze various metrics related to your website's traffic, including:

Number of visitors and pageviews

Bounce rate

Time on site

Traffic sources

Conversion rates

To use Google Analytics, you'll need to create an account and add a tracking code to your website. Once this is done, you'll be able to access a dashboard that shows you all of the metrics mentioned above and more.

Analyzing and interpreting data

Analyzing your website's data can be overwhelming, especially if you're new to SEO. However, there are a few key metrics that you should focus on when analyzing your data:

Organic traffic: This is the number of visitors who come to your website from search engines. Organic traffic is a good indicator of how well your website is ranking in search engine results pages (SERPs).

Bounce rate: This is the percentage of visitors who leave your website after viewing only one page. A high bounce rate can indicate that your website is not engaging enough or that visitors are not finding what they're looking for.

Conversion rate: This is the percentage of visitors who complete a desired action on your website, such as making a purchase or filling out a contact form. A low conversion rate may indicate that your website's content or design needs improvement.

Click-through rate (CTR): This is the percentage of clicks your website receives from search engine results pages (SERPs). A high CTR indicates that your website's title tags and meta descriptions are compelling and relevant to searchers.

Creating reports

Creating regular reports is important for tracking your progress and identifying areas for improvement. You can create reports manually using data from Google Analytics or use SEO reporting tools to automate the process.

When creating reports, it's important to focus on the metrics that matter most to your business goals. For example, if your goal is to increase sales, you should track metrics such as conversion rate and revenue generated.

Conclusion

Analyzing your website's data is essential to understanding how your SEO efforts are performing and making informed decisions on how to improve them. By tracking key metrics such as organic traffic, bounce rate, conversion rate, and click-through rate, and creating regular reports, you can gain valuable insights into your website's performance and make data-driven decisions.

Setting up Google Analytics

Setting up Google Analytics involves creating a Google Analytics account and adding a tracking code to your website. Here are the steps:

Sign up for a Google Analytics account at https://analytics.google.com/.

Click on "Admin" and create a new account, property, and view for your website.

Choose the type of property you want to track, such as a website or a mobile app.

Enter your website details and select your time zone.

Get your tracking code by clicking on the "Tracking Info" tab and then "Tracking Code." Copy the code.

Paste the tracking code into the header of every page on your website.

Verify that Google Analytics is working properly by checking the Real-Time reports in your account.

Once you have set up Google Analytics, you can track various metrics such as website traffic, user behavior, and conversions. This data can be used to make informed decisions about your SEO and digital marketing strategies.

Understanding website traffic and user behavior

Understanding website traffic and user behavior involves analyzing data collected through website analytics tools like Google Analytics. This data provides insights into how visitors interact with a website, which pages are most popular, how long they stay on each page, and where they are coming from. These insights can help website owners make informed decisions about their SEO strategy, content creation, and user experience.

Some important metrics to track include:

Sessions: The number of visits to your website.

Pageviews: The total number of pages viewed during a session.

Average session duration: The average length of time a user spends on your site.

Bounce rate: The percentage of visitors who leave your website after viewing only one page.

Exit rate: The percentage of visitors who leave your website after viewing a particular page.

Conversion rate: The percentage of visitors who complete a desired action, such as making a purchase or filling out a form.

By tracking and analyzing these metrics, website owners can gain a deeper understanding of their audience and how to optimize their website for better user engagement and conversions.

Measuring SEO success

Measuring SEO success involves tracking the performance of your website and its content in search engine results pages (SERPs) and analyzing the impact of SEO strategies on various metrics such as organic traffic, search engine ranking positions, bounce rates, click-through rates, and conversions.

To measure SEO success, you can use tools like Google Analytics, Google Search Console, and other SEO analytics tools that provide detailed reports on website traffic, user behavior, and search engine rankings. You can also set up custom goals and track conversions to measure the impact of your SEO efforts on your website's revenue and ROI.

It's important to regularly review and analyze your website's performance metrics to identify areas for improvement and optimize your SEO strategy accordingly. By measuring and analyzing SEO metrics, you can gain insights into your audience's behavior, preferences, and needs, and adjust your content and marketing tactics to better meet their needs and drive more traffic and revenue to your website.

Creating SEO reports

Creating SEO reports involves compiling and analyzing data related to website traffic, keyword rankings, backlinks, and other metrics to assess the performance of your SEO strategy. The report should clearly outline the key metrics and provide insights and recommendations to improve the website's search engine visibility.

When creating an SEO report, consider including the following elements:

Executive Summary: A brief overview of the report's findings and recommendations.

Key Metrics: An overview of the website's performance metrics such as organic traffic, keyword rankings, backlinks, and conversion rates.

Traffic Analysis: A breakdown of the website's traffic sources, including organic, paid, social, and referral traffic.

Keyword Analysis: An overview of the website's keyword performance, including keyword rankings, search volume, and competition.

Backlink Analysis: An analysis of the website's backlink profile, including the number and quality of backlinks and their impact on search engine rankings.

Competitor Analysis: A comparison of the website's performance metrics against its top competitors.

Recommendations: A list of actionable recommendations to improve the website's search engine visibility, such as optimizing content, building more high-quality backlinks, and improving website speed and user experience.

By regularly creating and reviewing SEO reports, you can gain insights into your website's performance, identify areas for improvement, and adjust your strategy accordingly to achieve better search engine visibility and drive more traffic to your website.

Chapter 10: Advanced SEO Techniques

In this chapter, we will explore some advanced SEO techniques that can take your website's visibility and rankings to the next level. These techniques are more complex and require a deeper understanding of SEO principles and strategies.

International SEO: If you have a website that targets audiences in different countries and languages, international SEO is essential. This involves optimizing your website for different languages and countries, including creating localized content, implementing hreflang tags, and using country-specific domain extensions.

Voice Search Optimization: With the rise of voice assistants like Alexa and Siri, optimizing your website for voice search queries is becoming increasingly important. This includes using natural language in your content, optimizing for long-tail keywords, and improving website speed and performance.

Featured Snippets Optimization: Featured snippets are brief answers to search queries that appear at the top of search engine results pages (SERPs). Optimizing your content to appear as a featured snippet can increase your website's visibility and traffic. This involves identifying common search queries related to your content, formatting your content in a way that matches the featured snippet format, and using schema markup to provide additional information.

Artificial Intelligence (AI) and Machine Learning (ML) in SEO: AI and ML are transforming the way we approach SEO. With AI-powered tools, you can analyze data, optimize content, and improve website performance more efficiently. AI and ML can also help you identify and target new keywords, create content that resonates with your audience, and improve user experience on your website.

Mobile-First Indexing: With the majority of internet traffic coming from mobile devices, Google has switched to a mobile-first indexing approach. This means that Google uses the mobile version of your website as the primary version for indexing and ranking purposes. Optimizing your website for mobile devices, including responsive design, fast loading times, and mobile-friendly content, is essential for SEO success.

By implementing these advanced SEO techniques, you can stay ahead of the competition and improve your website's visibility, traffic, and rankings. However, it's important to remember that SEO is an ongoing process that requires continuous optimization and improvement.

Advanced keyword research strategies

Advanced keyword research strategies can help you to identify new opportunities and gain a competitive edge. Here are some techniques that you can use:

Competitor Analysis: Analyze your competitors' websites to see what keywords they are targeting and how they are using them. Use tools like SEMrush or Ahrefs to find out which keywords they are ranking for, and try to identify gaps in their strategy that you can exploit.

Long-tail Keywords: Long-tail keywords are longer, more specific phrases that people use when they are searching for something. These keywords tend to have lower search volumes, but they are also less competitive. By targeting long-tail keywords, you can attract more qualified traffic to your website.

Keyword Clustering: Keyword clustering involves grouping related keywords together into clusters. By doing this, you can create content that targets multiple keywords at once, and improve the relevance and quality of your content.

Semantic SEO: Semantic SEO is a technique that involves using related keywords and synonyms to help search engines understand the meaning of your content. By including related terms in your content, you can improve your chances of ranking for a wider range of keywords.

Keyword Intent: Keyword intent refers to the reason why someone is searching for a particular keyword. By understanding the intent behind a keyword, you can create content that better meets the needs of your audience. For example, if someone is searching for "best running shoes for women," they are likely looking to buy shoes, so you could create content that compares different types of shoes or provides buying guides.

These advanced keyword research strategies can help you to uncover new opportunities and improve your SEO strategy. However, it's important to remember that SEO is an ongoing process, and you should continue to monitor and adjust your strategy as needed.

Semantic search and latent semantic indexing (LSI)

Semantic search refers to the process of understanding the meaning of words in the context of a search query and the intent behind it, rather than just matching keywords. It is a more sophisticated way of interpreting user queries and delivering relevant results based on the context of the search.

Latent semantic indexing (LSI) is a technique used by search engines to identify the relationship between different words and concepts within a piece of content. LSI allows search engines to understand the topic of the content better and deliver more relevant results to users. This technique involves analyzing the frequency and distribution of related words and phrases within a document to determine its overall theme and context. LSI can help in identifying long-tail keywords and optimizing content for better search visibility.

Voice search optimization

Voice search optimization is the process of optimizing your website and content to rank higher in voice search results. With the increasing popularity of voice assistants like Amazon's Alexa, Google Assistant, and Apple's Siri, voice search is becoming an important aspect of SEO. To optimize for voice search, you need to focus on conversational keywords and long-tail phrases that people are likely to use when speaking to a virtual assistant. You also need to ensure that your website is mobile-friendly, loads quickly, and has clear, concise content that answers common questions related to your business or industry. Additionally, it's important to claim your Google My Business listing and optimize it for local search, as voice assistants often prioritize local results when answering queries.

Machine learning and AI in SEO

Machine learning and artificial intelligence (AI) are playing an increasingly important role in the field of SEO. With the massive amount of data that search engines like Google are processing, AI algorithms are being used to analyze and understand this data more effectively, leading to more accurate search results.

One application of machine learning in SEO is in the development of algorithms that can identify patterns in search queries and predict user intent more accurately. This can help businesses optimize their content and website to better match user intent, leading to higher rankings and more relevant traffic.

Another area where AI is being used in SEO is in the development of natural language processing (NLP) models that can better understand the context and meaning of text on websites. This can help search engines like Google better understand the content of a website and determine its relevance to search queries.

Overall, as AI and machine learning continue to advance, we can expect to see even more sophisticated SEO strategies and techniques emerging in the future.

Future of SEO

The future of SEO is constantly evolving as search engines continue to update their algorithms and technology advances. Some of the trends that are likely to shape the future of SEO include:

Voice search: As more people use voice assistants such as Alexa and Google Assistant, optimizing content for voice search will become more important.

Mobile-first indexing: As more people use mobile devices to access the internet, search engines are placing more emphasis on mobile-friendly websites.

Artificial intelligence: Machine learning and AI are already being used by search engines to better understand user intent and deliver more personalized results.

Local SEO: With the rise of location-based searches, local SEO will become more important for businesses with physical locations.

Video content: Video content is becoming more popular, and search engines are starting to give it more weight in search results.

User experience: Search engines are increasingly prioritizing websites that provide a good user experience, with fast loading times and easy navigation.

As the world of SEO continues to evolve, businesses will need to stay up-to-date with the latest trends and best practices to stay competitive in search rankings.

Chapter 11: Common SEO Mistakes to Avoid

As important as it is to know what to do in SEO, it's also important to know what not to do. Here are some common SEO mistakes that should be avoided:

Keyword stuffing: Overloading your content with too many keywords can lead to penalties from search engines.

Neglecting mobile optimization: With the majority of internet traffic coming from mobile devices, it's crucial to ensure that your website is optimized for mobile use.

Ignoring meta tags: Title tags and meta descriptions are still important for SEO and should not be neglected.

Focusing only on search engines: While it's important to optimize for search engines, it's equally important to focus on providing a positive user experience for your audience.

Neglecting social media: Social media can be a powerful tool for driving traffic to your website and improving your SEO.

Using black hat tactics: Black hat tactics, such as buying backlinks or keyword stuffing, may provide short-term gains, but they can lead to penalties and long-term damage to your website's reputation.

Neglecting website security: Ensuring that your website has a secure connection (HTTPS) is not only important for user trust, but it's also a ranking factor for Google.

Ignoring analytics: Monitoring your website's analytics can provide valuable insights into your audience's behavior and help you make informed decisions about your SEO strategy.

By avoiding these common SEO mistakes, you can ensure that your website is optimized for both search engines and your audience, leading to improved rankings and a better user experience.

Keyword stuffing

Keyword stuffing is the practice of excessively using a particular keyword or keyphrase in an attempt to manipulate search engine rankings. This is a common SEO mistake that website owners make, as they believe that repeating a keyword several times will improve their website's ranking. However, search engines are now smarter and can recognize when content is over-optimized for a particular keyword.

Keyword stuffing can lead to penalties and harm the website's search engine rankings, as search engines prioritize high-quality content that is relevant to the user's search intent. Instead, it's essential to focus on creating high-quality content that satisfies the user's search intent and includes relevant keywords and phrases naturally.

Duplicate content

Duplicate content refers to blocks of content that are identical or substantially similar to each other, either within the same website or across multiple websites. It is important to avoid duplicate content because search engines may not be able to determine which version of the content to index, and this can negatively impact your website's search engine rankings. To avoid this, ensure that all pages on your website have unique, high-quality content that provides value to your users. You can also use canonical tags to specify which version of the content you want search engines to index.

Ignoring mobile optimization

Ignoring mobile optimization is a common SEO mistake to avoid. With the increasing number of mobile users, optimizing your website for mobile devices is essential for providing a good user experience and improving your search engine rankings. Ignoring mobile optimization can lead to slow page load times, difficult navigation, and poor user experience, which can ultimately lead to a decrease in traffic and rankings. To avoid this mistake, make sure to use responsive design, optimize images and videos for mobile devices, and prioritize mobile user experience in your website design and development.

Neglecting user experience

Neglecting user experience is a common SEO mistake to avoid. User experience plays a critical role in determining how long visitors stay on your website and whether they return. Neglecting user experience can lead to high bounce rates, low engagement, and poor search engine rankings. To avoid this mistake, make sure your website is easy to navigate, loads quickly, has high-quality content that is easy to read and understand, and provides a positive overall user experience. Additionally, ensure that your website is mobile-friendly, as more and more people are using mobile devices to access the internet.

Black hat SEO techniques

Black hat SEO techniques refer to unethical or deceptive practices that violate search engine guidelines to improve website rankings. These techniques include keyword stuffing, cloaking, hidden text, link farms, and other tactics that attempt to manipulate search engine algorithms. While these tactics may provide short-term gains in rankings, they can result in penalties or even permanent removal from search engine results pages. Therefore, it's important to avoid black hat techniques and focus on ethical and sustainable SEO strategies for long-term success.

Chapter 12: Conclusion

In conclusion, SEO is a crucial part of any digital marketing strategy. By optimizing your website for search engines, you can increase your online visibility and attract more organic traffic to your site. However, SEO is a complex and ever-evolving field, and it requires ongoing effort and attention to stay ahead of the competition.

To succeed in SEO, it's important to follow best practices, avoid common mistakes, and stay up to date with the latest trends and techniques. This guide has covered a wide range of topics related to SEO, from keyword research and on-page optimization to link building and analytics.

By following the advice and strategies outlined in this guide, you can improve your website's ranking in search engine results pages and achieve your online marketing goals. Whether you're a small business owner, an e-commerce site manager, or a digital marketing professional, SEO can help you reach your target audience and grow your online presence.

Recap of key SEO concepts

Sure, here's a recap of key SEO concepts covered in this guide:

SEO (Search Engine Optimization) is the practice of optimizing a website to improve its ranking in search engine results pages (SERPs) and increase organic traffic.

On-page optimization refers to optimizing the content and structure of a website's individual pages, while off-page optimization involves building links and online reputation to improve the website's authority.

Keyword research is the process of identifying keywords and phrases that potential customers use to find products or services related to a particular business or industry.

Technical SEO involves optimizing the technical aspects of a website, including site speed, architecture, schema markup, and more.

Local SEO is a strategy that helps businesses optimize their online presence for local search results, such as Google Maps listings.

E-commerce SEO is a strategy that helps online retailers optimize their product pages and category pages for better search engine rankings.

Content marketing is the process of creating and promoting valuable content to attract and engage a target audience.

Google Analytics is a web analytics tool that provides insights into website traffic, user behavior, and more.

Advanced SEO techniques include semantic search, voice search optimization, and machine learning.

Common SEO mistakes to avoid include keyword stuffing, duplicate content, neglecting mobile optimization, ignoring user experience, and using black hat SEO techniques.

Overall, effective SEO requires a combination of on-page optimization, off-page optimization, technical optimization, local optimization, e-commerce optimization, content marketing, and data analysis to continually improve website visibility, attract new customers, and grow business.

Importance of ongoing SEO efforts

Ongoing SEO efforts are crucial for maintaining and improving a website's search engine rankings. SEO is not a one-time fix, but a continuous process that requires consistent updates and optimizations to keep up with the ever-evolving search algorithms and user behavior. Without ongoing SEO efforts, a website may experience a decline in rankings, traffic, and ultimately, revenue. By regularly monitoring and adjusting SEO strategies, businesses can stay ahead of the competition and continue to attract and retain organic traffic.

Staying up-to-date with SEO trends and changes

Staying up-to-date with SEO trends and changes is crucial for any business or website owner. The world of SEO is constantly evolving, with search engines regularly updating their algorithms and introducing new features. To stay ahead of the competition, it's essential to keep up with these changes and adapt your SEO strategies accordingly.

One way to stay up-to-date is to regularly read industry blogs and news sources, attend SEO conferences and webinars, and network with other SEO professionals. It's also important to regularly review your website's analytics and search engine rankings to identify any changes or trends that may require adjustments to your SEO strategies.

By staying up-to-date with SEO trends and changes, you can ensure that your website remains visible and competitive in search engine rankings, driving traffic and business success.